BOOKS BY **ROBERT E. DALEY**

A Case for "Threes"
A Simple Plan . . . of Immense Complexity
Armour, Weapons, And Warfare
from Everlasting to Everlasting
Killer Sex
Life or Death, Heaven or Hell, You Choose!
Raptures and Resurrections
Short Tales
So . . . What Happens to the Package?
Study and Interpretation of The Scriptures Made Simple
Surviving Destruction as A Human Being
The Gospel of John
The Gospel of John (Red Edition)
The League of The Immortals
The New Testament - Pauline Revelation
The New Testament - Pauline Revelation Companion
"The World That Then Was . . ." & The Genesis That Now Is
What Color Are You?
What Makes A Christian Flaky?
What Really Happened to Judas Iscariot?
Who YOU Are in Christ . . . RIGHT NOW!

The Enhancement Series

> #1 Book of Ecclesiastes
> #2 Book of Daniel
> #3 Book of Romans
> #4 Book of Galatians
> #5 Book of Hebrews

The Deeper Things of God Series

> #1 The Personage of God
> #2 The Personage of Man
> #3 The Personage of Christ

The Enhancement Series• Book Five

THE NEW TESTAMENT

BOOK OF HEBREWS

EXPLOSIVELY
ENHANCED

This is an independent work, utilizing the
King James Translation of the Bible, with author
enhancement for clarity and presentation of intended thought.

Robert E. Daley

The Larry Czerwonka Company, LLC
Hilo, Hawai'i

First Edition — November 2014

This book is set in 14-point Garamond

Published by: The Larry Czerwonka Company,
LLChttp://thelarryczerwonkacompany.com

Printed in the United States of America

ISBN: 0692330143
ISBN-13: 978-0692330142

All scriptures used in this work are taken from the
King James Version of the Scriptures.

Introduction

The sole purpose for enhancement is for simple clarity.

In this work, the King James Translation of the Bible is unchanged within its textual record. Punctuation and translator added words may be altered, but the singular purpose behind that, is for clear understanding of intended divine thought by the reader.

Since the book is a major doctrinal thesis concerning the Law verses grace, it is important that the student of the word of God have a clear cognizance of spiritual truth. Drastic spiritual changes occurred upon the resurrection of the New Creation Lord, Jesus Christ of Nazareth. Those changes are largely unknown, or at the least, unrecognized by modern day Christianity, and may be clearly seen here.

This work presents the reality that there are now three separate "types" of Human Beings in existence, that are now living here on this planet, Earth. These three "types" of Human-Beings are: the *Gentile*, the *Jew*, and the *New Creation*.

Failure to understand this reality, will lead to spiritual confusion, and religious insistence. Division will be the end result, just as was the case in the scriptural letter that was addressed to the Corinthian church.

This author desires that all Christians become fully aware of who they are now "in Christ", after having asked Jesus of Nazareth to "save" them, and then direct them by his Holy Spirit, in their walk with God.

THE BOOK OF
HEBREWS

CHAPTER 1

1. God, *the Father of all of creation,* who at *various and* sundry times and in *various and* divers manners spake *clearly* in time past unto the *patriarch* fathers *of Israel,* by the *various* prophets *that he raised up,*

2. Hath in these last *probationary* days *of Humanity itself,* spoken unto us *directly* by his *Only Begotten* Son, whom he hath appointed, *after his resurrection from the dead, as the* heir of all things, *and* by whom also, he *originally, in the beginning,* made the worlds.

3. Who being, *within his humanity,* the *very* brightness of his glory, and the express*ed, exact* image of his person, and *while* upholding all things by the word of his power, when he had *all* by himself purged our sins *through his finished work upon the cross of Calvary,* sat down on the right hand of the *Father God in heaven, who is the* Majesty on high.

4. Being made *in his humanity,* so much better than the angels, as he hath by *the process of* inheritance obtained a*much* more excellent name than they . . . *and that is the name of MAN.*

5. For unto which of the angels said he at any time, "Thou art my son, this day have I begotten thee?" *(Psalms 2:7)* **And again, "I will be to him a Father, and he shall be to me a Son?"** *(II Samuel 7:14)*

6. **And again, when he** *first* **bringeth in the first begotten** *from the spiritual and physical dead, back* **into the world, he saith, "And let all the angels of God worship him."** *(Septuagint — Deuteronomy 32:43)*

7. **And of the** *holy* **angels** *themselves* **he saith, "Who maketh his angels spirits, and his ministers a flame of fire."** *(Psalms 104:4)*

8. **But unto the** *Only Begotten* **Son he saith, "Thy** *Kingdom of Heaven* **throne, O God, is for ever and ever.** *And* **a scepter of righteousness is the scepter of thy kingdom.**

9. *For* **thou hast** *truly* **loved righteousness, and hated iniquity. Therefore,** *because of that, the living* **God, even thy God, hath anointed thee with the oil of gladness above thy fellows."** *(Psalms 45:6-7)*

10. **And, Thou, Lord, in the beginning** *of the creation of all things,* **hast laid the foundation of the earth. And** *all of* **the** *three* **heavens** *that have been created,* **are the works of thine hands.**

11. **They shall perish** *within the passage of time***; but thou remainest; and they all shall wax old as doth a garment,** *but thou shalt continue for ever.*

12. **And as** *one does with* **a** *cloth* **vesture, shalt thou fold them up, and** *through a renovation by fire,* **they**

shall be changed. But thou art the same, and thy years shall not fail.

13.   But to which of the *lesser-creation-category* angels said he at any time, "Sit on my right hand, until I make thine enemies thy footstool?" *(Psalms 110:1)*

14.   Are they not all *angelic* ministering spirits, sent forth *at the direction of the Lord,* to minister *unto, and especially* for, them who shall be*come the* heirs of salvation?

CHAPTER 2

1.   Therefore, we ought to *pay attention and* give the more earnest heed to the things which we have heard *from those who have gone on before us,* lest at any time we should *forget the reality of spiritual truth, and* let them slip *away.*

2.   For if the word *of rebellion that was* spoken by*disobedient* angels was *ultimately* stedfast *and unrepented of,* and every *action of* transgression and disobedience received a just recompence of *judgmental* reward;

3.   How shall we *then* escape *certain destruction,* if we neglect so great *an offer of* salvation. Which at the first, *came to light and* began to be spoken *of* by the Lord *Jesus,* and was *then* confirmed unto us by them that *walked with him, and* heard him *teach.*

4.   God *the Father* also bearing them witness, both with signs and wonders, and with divers miracles, and *with Merismos* gifts *to align the soul of man; which were given* of the Holy Ghost, according to his own will?

5.   For unto the *lesser-creation-category, holy* angels *of the Most High God,* hath he not put in*to* subjection the world to come, whereof we speak. *Even though Adam became a servant to whom he obeyed* (Romans 6:16), *nevertheless that did not alter the status or position that Man was originally created for.*

6.   But one *man named David,* in a certain place *within the psalms* testified, saying, "What is *this creature called* Man, that thou art mindful of him? or *even* the son of man, that thou visitest him?

7.   Thou hast made him a little lower than the *Holy Godhead known of as* Elohim. Thou *hath* crownedst him with glory and honour, and *authoritatively* didst set him over *all of* the works of thy hands.

8.   Thou hast *purposely* put all *created* things in subjection under his feet." *(Psalms 8:4-8)* For in that he put all *things* in subjection under him, he left nothing that is not put under him, *except for the Creator God himself, and his throne. (I Corinthians 15:27)* But *right* now we see not yet all things *manifestly* put under

him, *because we are still operating within the Probationary Period.*

9. But we see *his Only Begotten Son* **Jesus, who was made** *in his humanity* **a little lower than the** *lesser-creation-category, holy* **angels for the** *purpose of the* **suffering of** *spiritual* **death,** *and then magnificently* **crowned with glory and honour** *upon his resurrection from that death.* **That he** *alone,* **by the grace of God, should taste** *of spiritual* **death for every man.**

10. For it became him, for whom are all things, and by whom are all things, in bringing many *adopted* sons unto glory, to make the captain of their salvation, *Christ Jesus,* perfect through sufferings.

11. For both he that sanctifieth *and sets apart,* and they who are *to be* sanctified, are all of one *mystical body.* For which cause he is not ashamed to call them *his* brethren,

12. Saying, "I will declare thy name *O God* unto my brethren, in the midst of the church will I sing praise unto thee." *(Psalms 22:22)*

13. And again *he saith,* "I will put my trust in him." *(II Samuel 22:3)* And again, "Behold I and the children *of the Most High* which *the* God *of all grace* hath given *unto* me." *(Isaiah 8:18)*

14. Forasmuch then as *those who shall become* the children *of the Most High God* are partakers of *the two elements of* flesh and blood, he also himself likewise took part of the same *when he took upon himself the flesh part*. That through *the partaking of spiritual* death he might destroy him that had the power of *both spiritual and physical* death, that is, the devil.

15. And *should finally* deliver them who through fear of *that* death were all their lifetime subject to *the* bondage *of sin*.

16. For verily he took not on *himself the nature of* the *lesser-creation-category, holy* angels, but he took *up*on *himself* the *promised* seed of *Humanity, for covenant purposes, which finds its origin in* Abraham.

17. Wherefore in all things it behooved him to be made like unto his brethren*in every respect*, that he might be *fully* a human man, *and* a merciful and faithful High Priest, *when the time came*, in things *pertaining* to God, to make reconciliation for the sins of the people.

18. For in that he himself hath suffered being tempted *while he was on this earth*, he is *now* able to succor *and comfort* them that are tempted *in a manner like as he was*.

CHAPTER 3

1. Wherefore, *my* holy brethren, *who are* partakers of the heavenly *high* calling *of God*, consider *if*

you will the Apostle and High Priest of our profession, Christ Jesus.

2.　Who was faithful to him that *had* appointed him, as also Moses was *faithful unto God* in all *of* his house.

3.　For this *genuine, human* man was counted worthy of *receiving much* more glory than Moses *did,* inasmuch as he who *is the one who* hath builded the house, hath *much* more honour than the house *itself.*

4.　For every house is, *by design,* builded by some man, but he that *originally* built all things *is the living* God.

5.　And Moses verily *was* faithful in all *of* his house, *which is the Nation of Israel,* as a servant *of God. This he did* for a testimony *and an example* of those things which were to be spoken *of* after*ward.*

6.　But Christ *Jesus our Lord is faithful* as a *family-member* son over his own house. Whose *spiritual* house are we, if we hold fast the confidence and the rejoicing of the hope *that we have,* firm unto the end.

7.　Wherefore as the Holy Ghost saith *in the Scriptures*, "Today if ye will hear his voice,

8.　Harden not your hearts, as in the provocation, in the day of temptation in the wilderness.

9.　When your *patriarch* fathers tempted me, *and* proved me, and saw my works *for* forty years."
(Psalms 95:7-11)

10.   Wherefore I was grieved with that generation *that wandered in the wilderness*, and said, "They do
always err in *their* heart, and they have not known
my ways.

11.   So I sware in my wrath, *that* they shall not
enter into my *prepared* rest." *(Septuagint — Psalms 95:8)*

12.   Take heed, *my* brethren, lest there be *develop-
ing* in any of you an evil heart of unbelief, in departing from the living God.

13.   But *continue to* exhort one another daily, while
it is *still* called Today. Lest any of you *should* be
hardened *in your heart* through the deceitfulness of
sin.

14.   For we are made partakers of Christ, *only* if
we hold the beginning of our confidence steadfast
unto the end.

15.   While it is said *within the Scriptures*, "Today if
ye will hear his voice, harden not your hearts, as
in the provocation." *(Psalms 95:7-8)*

16.   For some *of those belonging to covenant Israel, even*
when they had heard *from God*, did provoke. How-
beit not all *of the people* that came out of Egypt by
Moses *moved to provoke the Lord*.

17.   But with whom was he grieved *for* forty
years, *because of their bad behavior*? *Was it* not with
them that had *willfully disobeyed, and* sinned, whose
carcasses *ultimately* fell in the wilderness?

18. And to whom sware he that they should not enter into his *prepared* rest, but to them that believed not? So we see that they could not enter in*to what God had provided for them* because of *their persistent*
unbelief.

CHAPTER 4

1. Let us therefore *take heed and* fear, lest, a promise *from God* being left *unto us* of entering into his *prepared* rest, any of you should seem to come short of it.
2. For unto us was the gospel preached, as well as unto them, but the word *that was* preached *unto them* did not profit them, not being mixed with faith in them that heard *it.*
3. For we which have believed *on the finished work of the cross of Jesus* do enter into *the* rest *that he has provided,* as he said, "As I have sworn in my wrath, if they shall enter into my rest." *(Psalms 95:11)* Although the works *of this rest* were finished, *because of foreknowledge,* from *before* the foundation of the world.
4. For he spake in *the Scriptures at* a certain place, of the *significance of the* seventh *day* on this wise, "And God did rest the seventh day from all *of* his works." *(Genesis 2:2-3)*

5.   And in this *place* again, "If they shall enter into my rest." *(Psalms 95:7-11)*

6.   Seeing therefore it remaineth that some must enter therein, and they *of the Nation of Israel,* to whom it was first preached, entered not in because of unbelief.

7.   Again, he limiteth a certain day, saying in David, "Today, after so long a time" . . . as it is said, "Today, if ye will hear his voice, harden not your hearts." *(Psalms 95:7-8)*

8.   For if Jesus, *that is, Joshua,* had given them rest *after they had gone into the promised land,* then would he not afterward have spoken of another day *through the psalmist.*

9.   There remaineth therefore *even unto this day* a rest *that has been prepared* to *and for* the people of God.

10.   For *whomsoever* he *is,* that is entered into his *prepared* rest, he also hath ceased from *the labour of* his own works, *even* as God *did* rest from his *restoration work.* *(Genesis 2:2)*

11.   Let us *purpose then to* labour therefore, to enter into that rest *that God has provided for all men through the finished work of Christ Jesus,* lest any man *should* fall *away* after the same example of unbelief *that we saw happen unto the wandering generation of the Nation of Israel.*

12.   For the *living* word of God *is* quick, and powerful, and sharper than any two-edged sword.

Piercing even to the dividing asunder of *a man's* soul and *his* spirit, *through the merismos giftings of the Holy Spirit of God.* And *it is a divider* of the *spiritual* joint*s* and *the life giving* marrow. And *it is* a discerner *even* of the thoughts and *the* intents of the *depths of the* heart.

13. Neither is there any creature *in existence* that is not *revealed and* manifest in his sight. But all *created* things *are* naked and opened unto the eyes of him with whom we have to do.

14. Seeing then that *today* we have a great High Priest, that is *gone before us and* passed into the heavens, Jesus *of Nazareth* the Son of *the living* God, let us hold fast *to our* profession.

15. For we have not an High Priest which *is distant, and* cannot be touched with the feeling of our infirmities. But *he* was *himself* in all points, tempted like as *we are, yet* without sin.

16. Let us therefore come boldly *and confidently, through fervent prayer, even* unto the throne of grace *in heaven,* that we may obtain *the* mercy *that is available,* and find *the* grace *of God* to help *us* in *a* time of need.

CHAPTER 5

1.   For every *ministering* **High Priest,** *that is* **taken from among men,** *within the Nation of Israel,* **is ordained for** *other* **men in things** *pertaining* **to God, that he may offer** *up* **both gifts** *of thanksgivings* **and sacrifices for** *the* **sins** *that have been committed.*

2.   **Who can have compassion on the ignorant,** *and the less fortunate,* **and on them that are out of the way, for that he himself also is** *personally* **compassed** *about* **with infirmity.**

3.   **And by reason** *of his shortcomings* **hereof, he ought, as** *he does* **for the people, so** *he needs to do* **also for himself, to offer** *unto God a blood sacrifice* **for sins.**

4.   **And no man taketh this** *priestly* **honour unto himself, but** *only* **he that is called of God, as** *was Moses' brother* **Aaron.**

5.   **So also** *in like manner,* **Christ glorified not himself to be made an High Priest, but he that** *originally* **said unto him, "Thou art my Son, today have I begotten thee."** *(Psalms 2:7)*

6.   **As he saith also in another** *place within the psalms,* **"Thou** *art* **a** *High* **Priest for ever after the Order of Melchizedek."** *(Psalms 110:4)*

7.   **Who in the days of his flesh***ly walk on this earth,* **when he had offered up prayers and**

supplications, *within the Garden of Gethsemane,* with strong crying and tears unto him that was able to save him from *that heinous physical* death, and was heard in that he feared, *or more precisely dreaded what lay ahead.*

8.   Though he were a Son *of Man, and soon to be the Only Begotten Son of God,* yet learned he obedience by the *very* things which he suffered.

9.   And being made perfect *through his sufferings and death, upon his resurrection* he became the author of eternal salvation unto all them that *would* obey him.

10.   *Being* called of God a High Priest after the *established* Order of Melchizedek.

11.   Of whom we have many things to say, and *at this time* hard to be uttered, seeing *that* ye are *spiritually* dull of hearing.

12.   For when, for the time, ye ought to be *the* teachers *of spiritual things,* ye have need that *some other* one teach you *once* again which *be* the *very* first principles of the oracles of God, and are become such as have need of *spiritual* milk *yourself,* and not of strong *spiritual* meat.

13.   For every one that *continues to* useth *spiritual* milk *is* unskillful in *using* the word of righteousness, for he is *still* a babe *in Christ.*

14. But strong *spiritual* meat belongeth to them *who have studied, and* that are of full age, *even* those who by reason of us*ing them,* have *had* their *spiritual* senses exercised to discern *between* both good and evil.

CHAPTER 6

1. Therefore leaving *behind* the *foundational* principles of the doctrine of Christ, let us go on *within our daily walk with God* unto *spiritual maturity and* perfection. Not laying *once* again the foundation*al reality* of *genuine* repentance from *the* dead works *of the past,* and of *the exercising of gifted* faith toward God.

2. *Or of a striving over,* of the doctrine of *the seven* baptisms *that are mentioned within the Scriptures.* And *having a cognizance* of *the validity of ministering through the* laying on of hands. And *a working knowledge* of *the genuine truth concerning the* resurrection of the dead, and of *the sureties of* eternal judgment.

3. And this will we *purpose to* do, if God *shall* permit. *Which, of course, he will.*

4. For *I sadly testify unto you that it shall be* impossible for those *individuals from a Hebrew background,* who were once enlightened *because of a spiritual rebirth,* and have tasted of the heavenly gift *from God, of the forgiveness of their sins that are past,* and were made partakers of the Holy Ghost *by his recreating, indwelling presence,*

5. **And have tasted** *of* **the** *richness of the* **good word of God, and** *are made partakers of* **the powers of the world to come** *whereof we speak;*

6. **If they shall** *choose to* **fall away** *and make themselves a transgressor, by the building again of their trust in the things that once they destroyed; that is, the various aspects of the Mosaic Law. (Galatians 2:20) It shall be impossible I say,* **to renew them again unto** *genuine* **repentance, seeing** *that* **they** *knowingly, willingly, and consciously* **crucify** *un*to **themselves the Son of God afresh, and put him to an open shame** *by returning to the various aspects of that Mosaic Law which is unable to redeem a man's spirit. And it shall also hold true for individuals from a Gentile background, who have been redeemed through the new-birth, and then have returned to their own vomit, by not renewing their mind, (Romans 12:2) nor cleansing themselves of all filthiness of the flesh and the soul, (II Corinthians 7:1) and have not put off the old man which is corrupt according to the deceitful lusts, and put on the new man which is created in righteousness and true holiness, (Ephesians 4:22-24) and have not laid aside every weight and the sin which doth so easily beset them, (Hebrews 12:1) and have backslidden to such an extent, that they no longer believe in their heart unto righteousness, and have forsaken the truth, that Christ Jesus died for them.*

7.   For *just like* the earth which drinketh in the *blessing of the* rain that cometh oft upon it, and *it* bringeth forth herbs meet for them by whom it is dressed, *and ultimately will* receiveth *the* blessing *that cometh* from God.

8.   But *conversely,* that *portion of creation* which *sin has adversely affected, and that* beareth *nothing but* thorns and briars *is surely* rejected *at the time of the reckoning,* and *is* nigh unto cursing, whose *ultimate* end is to be burned. *So will those who have rejected the completed finished work that Jesus has provided, find themselves separated from a loving God, forevermore, and destined for the fires of Hell.*

9.   But, beloved, we are persuaded *that we shall hear of* better things of you, and *of those* things that accompany salvation *through faith in the finished work of Christ Jesus,* though we thus speak.

10.   For God *is* not unrighteous to forget your work and labour of love, which ye have shown toward his name, in that ye have ministered to the saints *through faith,* and do *yet continue to* minister.

11.   And we desire that every one of you do show the same diligence to the full assurance of hope *in Christ, right up* unto the *very* end.

12.   *And,* that ye be not slothful, but *rather* followers of them who through faith *in Christ,* and patience, inherit the promises *that God has made.*

13. For when God *originally* made *a* promise to Abraham, because he could swear by no*thing that was* greater, he sware by himself.

14. Saying, "Surely blessing I will bless thee, and multiplying I will multiply thee." *(Genesis 22:17)*

15. And so, after he had patiently endured *for twenty-five years*, he *finally* obtained the promise *of a son.*

16. For men *on this earth* verily swear by the greater *of the two*, and an oath *that has been written* for *agreed* confirmation *is* to them an end of all strife.

17. Wherein God *also*, willing more abundantly to show unto *those who would become* the heirs of *his* promise, the immutability of his counsel, confirmed *it* by a *written* oath *recorded within the Scriptures.*

18. That by two immutable things, *first, his verbal promise to Abraham, and then a Scriptural written oath*, in *the* which *it was* impossible for God to lie, we might have a strong consolation, who have fled *from the bondage of sin, and sought* for refuge *within the finished work of Christ*, to lay hold upon the *blessed* hope *that is* set before us *in Christ Jesus alone.*

19. Which *wonderful* **hope** we have as an *unmovable* anchor of the soul, *which is* both sure and steadfast, and which *even* entereth into that *which is* within the veil.

20. Whither the *blessed, holy,* forerunner is for us *already* entered, *even* Jesus *our Lord, who is now* made an High Priest forever*more* after the Order of Melchizedek.

CHAPTER 7

1. For this *aged man,* Melchizedek, *who was in reality the middle son of Noah,* was the king of *the city of* Salem; *and he was also the* priest of the Most High God *when no established Mosaic Law priesthood even existed.* Who *at the direction of God* met *the patriarch* Abraham *as he was* returning from the slaughter of *Chedorlaomer, and the kings that were with him at the valley of Shaveh, which is* the kings *valley.* And *Melchizedek* blessed him.

2. To whom also Abraham*, before the Law of Moses ever existed,* gave *the tithe, which is* a tenth part of all *of the spoils that he had obtained.* First, being by interpretation, *he is known of as the* King of righteousness, and after that *he is* also *known as the* King of Salem*, a city also known of today as Jerusalem,* which *name* is *by interpretation,* King of peace.

3. *Who at that time, because of his age of approximately 538 years, was* without *recorded* father, *and* without *recorded* mother, *and* without *recorded* descent, *seemingly* having neither beginning of days, nor end of life, but *was* made like unto the Son of God *himself. And as such, he is able to* abideth *as* a priest continually.

4. Now consider how great this *regular, common, human* man *named Shem* **was,** unto whom even the patriarch Abraham gave the tenth of the spoils *of all that he had obtained.*

5. And verily they that are of the sons of Levi, who *within the whole of the Aaronic Priesthood,* receive the *established* office of the priesthood *according to the Law of Moses,* have a commandment to take tithes of the people according to the *Mosaic* Law; that is, *to receive tithes* of their *own* brethren, *even* though they *also* come out of the loins of Abraham.

6. But *Melchizedek,* he whose descent *was not recorded, and who* is not counted *as coming* from them, received *the offered* tithes of Abraham, and *then turned around and* blessed him that had *received* the promises *from God.*

7. And without all contradiction the lesser *of the two* is *always* blessed of the better *of the two.*

8. And *currently,* here *on this earth* men that *physically* die *still* receive tithes *within the Aaronic Priesthood, even as it was established.* But there, *in heaven today,* he *personally* **receiveth them** of whom it is witnessed that he liveth, *even Jesus our High Priest.*

9. And as I may so say, Levi also, *the patriarch,* who received tithes, *originally* paid tithes in Abraham.

10. For he was yet *with*in the loins of his *great grand*-father, when Melchizedek met him.

11. If therefore *spiritual* perfection were *to come about* by the Levitical priesthood, for under it the *common* people received *all of the aspects of* the Law *of Moses, then* what further need *was there* that another priest should *a*rise *to minister* after the Order of Melchizedek, and not be called after the Order of Aaron?

12. For *if* the *root of the belief system, which is the-*priesthood, *is* being changed *by God, then* there is made, of necessity, a change also of the *reigning* Law *of Moses.*

13. For he of whom these things are spoken *of today,* pertaineth to another *Hebrew* tribe, of which no man *legally* gave *an* attendance at the altar *of sacrifice.*

14. For *it is quite* evident that our Lord *Jesus* sprang out of *the tribe of* Judah, of which tribe Moses spake nothing concerning *the* priesthood *when it was all originally established.*

15. And it is yet far more evident, for that after the similitude of Melchizedek, *the priest of God,* there ariseth another priest.

16. *One* who is made, not after the law of a carnal commandment, *as is contained within the Law of Moses,* but *rather* after the power of an endless life.

17. For he testifieth *in the psalms,* "Thou *art* a priest for ever after the Order of Melchizedek." *(Psalms 110:4)*

18. For there is verily a disannulling of the commandment *contained within the Law of Moses* **going before** *the heavenly appointment within the psalms,* **for the weakness and unprofitableness thereof.**

19. For the Law *of Moses* made nothing perfect. But the bringing in of a better hope *through the finished work of Christ Jesus upon the cross* **did,** by the which we *are able to* draw nigh unto God.

20. And inasmuch as not without an *confirming* oath, *he was made a High* Priest.

21. For those *other High* Priests, *under the Law of Moses,* were made *to be High Priests* without a *written* oath. But this *man Jesus, was made a High Priest* with a *written* oath by him that said unto him, "The Lord sware and will not repent, Thou *art* a *High* Priest for ever after the Order of Melchizedek." *(Psalms 110:4)*

22. *And* by so much *more also,* was Jesus made a surety of a *much* better *New* Testament.

23. And *indeed,* they truly were many *High* Priests, because they were not suffered, *or allowed,* to continue *in their priesthood ministry* by reason of *their own physical* death.

24. But this *man Jesus Christ,* because he continueth *to live for*ever, hath an unchangeable priesthood.

25. Wherefore, he is able also to save them to the uttermost that come*th* unto God by him, seeing *that* he ever liveth *as a High Priest* to make intercession for them.

26. For such an High Priest became us, *who is* holy, *and* harmless, *and* undefiled, *and* separate from sinners, and made higher than the heavens.

27. Who needeth not *on a* daily *basis*, as those *other* High Priests, to *have to* offer up *a* sacrifice, first for his own sins, and then for the people's *sins*. For this he did *only* once, when he offered up himself.

28. For the Law *of Moses* maketh men *to be* High Priests which have infirmity. But the word of the *written* oath, which was *given* since *the founding of* the Law *of Moses*, **maketh** the *Only Begotten* Son *a High Priest*, who is consecrated for evermore.

CHAPTER 8

1. Now of *all of* the things which we have spoken *about,* **this is** the sum: We *currently* have such a*n* High Priest, who is *presently* set on the right hand of the throne of the Majesty in the heavens.

2. *Who is* a minister of the *heavenly* sanctuary, and of the true tabernacle, which the Lord pitched, and not *of the tabernacle that was pitched by* man *on the earth.*

3. For every *active and operative* High Priest, is ordained to offer *both* gifts and sacrifices for sin.

Wherefore *it is* of necessity that this man have somewhat also to offer.

4.　For if he were *still living* on *the* earth, he should not be a *High* Priest, seeing that there are *already ordained High* Priests that offer gifts according to the Law *of Moses.*

5.　Who serve *only* unto the example and shadow of *the* heavenly things *themselves*, as Moses was admonished *and corrected* of God when he was about to make the tabernacle *in the wilderness*, for: "See," saith he, *"That* thou make all things according to the pattern *that was* shown *un*to thee in the mount."
(Exodus 25:9 & 40)

6.　But now hath he, *that is, Jesus,* obtained a more excellent ministry *than the other High Priests. And,* by how much *more* also he is the mediator of a *New and* better covenant *known as the Christian Blood Covenant*, which was established upon better promises.

7.　For if that first *covenant, between God and Abraham,* had been *perfect and* faultless, then should no place have *ever* been sought for the second.

8.　For finding *a* fault with them *because of their rebellion*, he saith, "Behold, the days come," saith the Lord, *"in the* which I will make a New *Blood* Covenant with *those from* the house of Israel and with *those from* the house of Judah *who will accept it.*

9.　Not according to the *blood* covenant that I made with *Abraham and with* their fathers, in the day when I took them by the hand to lead them out of the land of Egypt. Because they continued not in *obedience to* my covenant, and I regarded them not," saith the Lord.

10.   "For this is the *New Blood* Covenant that I will make with *those from* the house of Israel after those days," saith the Lord; "I will put my laws into their mind, and *I will* write them in their hearts *by the power of my Holy Spirit*, and I will be to them a God, and they shall be to me a people.

11.   And they shall not *need to* teach every man his neighbor, and *teach* every man his brother, saying, Know the Lord, for all *of the individuals that are within that Christian Blood Covenant* shall know me, from the least to the greatest.

12.   For I will be merciful to their unrighteousness, and their sins and their iniquities will I remember no more *because of the shed blood of my Only Begotten Son*." *(Jeremiah 31:31-34)*

13.   In that he saith, a New *Blood* **Covenant**, he hath made the first *one* old. Now *then*, that which decayeth and waxeth old *for the specific purpose of redemption, is* ready to vanish away.

CHAPTER 9

1.   Then verily the first *blood* **covenant** *with Abraham* had also *earthly* ordinances of divine service, and a worldly sanctuary *which was established through the Law of Moses.*

2.   For there was a*n earthly* tabernacle *that was* made. The first *tabernacle*, wherein *was* the candlestick, and the table, and the showbread. Which is *simply* called the sanctuary.

3.   And after the second veil *that had been hung*, the *innermost* tabernacle which is called the holiest of all.

4.   Which had *within it* the golden censer, and the ark of the covenant *chest, that was* overlaid round about with gold, wherein *was* the golden pot that had *fresh* manna, and Aaron's rod that budded *overnight*, and the *stone* tables of the covenant, *on which were written the Ten Commandments from God.*

5.   And over it the cherubim of glory shadowing the mercy seat *with their wings. The details* of which we cannot now speak particularly.

6.   Now when *all of* these things were thus ordained, the *regular* priests went always into the first tabernacle *only*, accomplishing the *requirements of the* service *of God.*

7.   But into the second, *innermost tabernacle,* **went** the High Priest alone, once every year. *And* not without *sacrificial* blood, which he offered *first* for himself, and *then* *for* the errors of the people.

8.   The Holy Ghost *with* this *tabernacle* signifying, that the way into the *genuine* holiest of all, *the Throne Room of God,* was not yet made *available and* manifest, while as the first *blood covenant* tabernacle was yet standing.

9.   Which *was* *only* a *foreshadowing* figure for the time then present. In *the* which were offered *once again,* both gifts *of worship* and sacrifices *for sins,* that could not make him that *actually* did the service perfect, as pertaining to the conscience.

10.   *But,* **which stood** only in *fleshly* meats and drinks, and divers washings, and *other* carnal ordinances, *that were* imposed *upon* ***them*** until the time of *the* reformation.

11.   But Christ *Jesus* being come an High Priest *after his resurrection* of good things to come, by a greater and more perfect tabernacle *of his body,* *which was* not made with hands, that is to say, *it is* not of this building *at all.*

12.   Neither by the *atonement* blood of goats and *of* calves, but by his own *precious, remission* blood, he entered in once into the holy place *in heaven,* having obtained eternal redemption *for us.*

13.   For if the *atonement* blood of bulls and of goats, and the *residue* ashes of a *sacrificial* heifer, sprinkling the unclean, *sufficiently* sanctifieth to the purifying of the flesh *here on this earth, under the Law of Moses*;

14.   How much more shall the *precious, remission* blood of Christ *Jesus*, who through the eternal *Holy* Spirit, offered himself without *any* spot *of offense* to *a holy* God, *then* purge your *very* conscience from *your valueless* dead works to *the intent, that ye might* serve the living God?

15.   And for this *very* cause, he is the mediator of the New Testament *that God has established.* That by means of *spiritual* death, for the redemption of the transgressions *that were* under the first *Old* Testament, they which are *"the* called*"* might receive the promise of eternal inheritance.

16.   For where a*ny* testament *is*, there must also of necessity, be the death of the testator.

17.   For a *legal, binding* testament *is only* of force after men *who are the testators* are dead. Otherwise it is of no strength at all while the testator *himself still* liveth.

18.   Whereupon neither the first *testament* was dedicated without blood.

19.   For when Moses had spoken every precept *of the word of God* to all *of* the people, according to

the *established* law, he took the *atonement* blood of calves and of goats, *along* with water, and *some blood-soaked* scarlet wool, and *some* hyssop, and sprinkled both the book, and all *of* the people.

20. Saying, "This *is* the *atonement* blood of the testament which God hath enjoined unto you." *(Exodus 24:4-8)*

21. Moreover he sprinkled with *the atonement* blood both the tabernacle, and all *of* the vessels *and utensils* of the ministry.

22. And almost all things are by the Law *of Moses,* purged with *atonement* blood. And without *the* shedding of *the remission* blood *of Christ Jesus, there* is *going to be* no remission *of the sins of Mankind.*

23. *It was* therefore *absolutely* necessary that the patterns *that Moses saw* of *the* things *that were* in the heavens should be purified with these *animal-blood sacrifices.* But the *very* heavenly things themselves *needed to be purified* with *much* better sacrifices than these.

24. For Christ *Jesus* is not entered into the *tabernacles of the* holy places *that are on this earth, and were* made with hands, **which are** *but* the figures of the true. But *rather* into *the Holy of Holies tabernacle in* heaven itself, now to appear in the presence of *the living* God for us.

25. Nor yet that he should *need to* offer himself often, as *is symbolized when* the High Priest *on earth*

entereth into the holy place every year with *the* blood of others.

26.   For then, must he often have suffered *shame and pain* since the foundation of the world. But now, once in the end of the world, hath he appeared to put away *the very Law of* Sin, by the sacrifice of himself.

27.   And as it is appointed *and ordained* unto men once to die *during the probation*, but after this *one death, to bring forth* the judgment,

28.   So Christ *Jesus* was once offered *in sacrifice* to bear the sins of many, and unto them that look for him *at both the Rapture and his Second Coming* shall he appear the second time without sin unto salvation.

CHAPTER 10

1.   For the *ceremonial portion of the* Law *of Moses* having a shadow of *the* good things *that were* to come, *and* not *actually expressing* the very image of the things, can never with those *innocent animal* sacrifices, which they offered year by year continually, make the comers thereunto perfect.

2.   For *if they were made perfect*, then would they not have *ceremonially* ceased to be offered? Because that the worshippers once purged *from those transgressions*,

should have had no more conscience of sins *from then on?*

3.　But in those *innocent animal* **sacrifices there is** *made* a remembrance again of sins every *single* year.

4.　For *it is* not *even* possible that the *atonement* blood of bulls and of goats *alone* should *be able to* take away *the* sins *of Human Beings completely.*

5.　Wherefore, when he cometh into the world, he saith *within the psalms*, "Sacrifice and offering thou wouldest not, but a body hast thou prepared me.

6.　In burnt offerings and *innocent animal* **sacrific-es**for sins thou hast had no pleasure."

7.　Then said I, "Lo, I come (in the volume of the book it is written of me) to do thy will, O God." *(Psalms 40:6-8)*

8.　Above when he said, "Sacrifice and offering and burnt offerings and *innocent animal* **offering** for sin thou wouldest not, neither hadst pleasure therein; which are offered by the *ceremonial portion of the* **Law** *of Moses.*"

9.　Then said he: "Lo, I come to do thy will, O God." *(Psalms 40:6-7)* He taketh away the First *Blood Covenant with its Mosaic Law and innocent animal sacrifices,* that he may establish the Second *Blood Covenant with the sacrifice of Christ Jesus, and the knowledge of the righteousness of God.*

10. By the which *perfect aspect of the* will *of God* *(Romans 12:2)* we are *now* sanctified *and uniquely set apart* through the offering of the *physical* body of Jesus Christ once *and for all.*

11. And every priest *that* standeth daily ministering and offering oftentimes the same *innocent animal* sacrifices, which can never take away sins, *does so in vain.*

12. But this man, *Christ Jesus*, after he had offered *just* one sacrifice for sins for ever *by the offering of himself*, sat down on the right hand of God.

13. From henceforth *he is fully* expecting *un*til *all of* his enemies *shall* be made his footstool.

14. For by one offering, *and one offering only*, he hath perfected for ever them that are sanctified *and set apart.*

15. *Whereof* the Holy Ghost also is a witness *of this work un*to us, for after that he had said before,

16. "This *is* the *Second Blood* Covenant that I will make with them after those days," saith the Lord; "I will put my laws into their hearts, and in their minds will I write them.

17. And their sins and *their* iniquities will I remember no more." *(Jeremiah 31:33-34)*

18. Now where *legal* remission of these *sins and iniquities* **is, there is** no more *need for an* offering for sin.

19.   Having *now* therefore, brethren, *the* boldness to *legally* enter into the holiest *tabernacle of all, in heaven,* by the *remission* blood of Jesus,

20.   By a *brand* new and living way, which he hath *personally* consecrated for us, through the veil, that is to say, his *very own* flesh;

21.   And *also having* an High Priest, *after the Order of Melchizedek,* over the *very* house*hold* of God;

22.   Let us *now* draw near with a true heart, in full assurance of faith, having our hearts sprinkled from an evil conscience *by the remission blood of Jesus,* and our *natural terrestrial* bodies washed with *the* pure water *of the word of God.*

23.   Let us hold fast the *declared* profession of *our* faith without wavering, for he *is* faithful that promised.

24.   And let us consider one another, *and purpose* to provoke *one another* unto love and to good works.

25.   Not forsaking the assembling of ourselves together, as the manner of some *is,* but *rather* exhorting *one another unto excellence.* And so much the more, as ye see the day *of his return* approaching.

26.   For if we *choose to* sin willfully, after that we have received the knowledge of the truth, there remaineth no more sacrifice for sins.

27. But a certain fearful looking for of judgment and fiery indignation, which shall devour
the adversaries *of God.*

28. *In the Old Testament* he that despised Moses'
law, *and rebelled and disobeyed,* died without mercy under *the testimony of* two or three witnesses.

29. Of how much sorer punishment, suppose
ye, shall he be thought worthy *of today,* who hath
trodden under foot the Son of God, and hath
counted the *precious remission* blood of the *Second Blood*
Covenant, wherewith he was sanctified, an unholy
thing, and hath done despite unto the Spirit of
grace *by not submitting himself to the righteousness of God,
and continueth to go about to establish his own righteousness?*
(Romans 10:3)

30. For we *claim to* know him that hath *definitively*
said, "Vengeance *belongeth* unto me, I will recompense", saith the Lord. *(Deuteronomy 32:35)*

31. *Consider that* it is a fearful thing to fall into the
hands of the living God.

32. But call to remembrance, *if ye will,* the former
days, in *the* which, after ye were illuminated *through*
the new-birth, ye endured a great fight of afflictions.

33. Partly, whilst ye were made a gazing stock
in front of others, both by reproaches and afflictions
that ye suffered, and partly, whilst ye became com-
panions of them that were *also* so used.

34. For ye had *demonstrated* compassion of me in my bonds, and *ye* took joyfully the spoiling of your *material* goods;knowing *with*in yourselves that ye have in heaven a better and a *more* enduring substance.

35. *I beseech thee, brethren,* cast not away therefore your *faith and* confidence *in the finished work of Christ,* which hath great recompense of reward.

36. For ye *simply* have need of patience *and confidence,* that, after ye have done the will of God, *even as did Abraham,* ye might receive the promise.

37. For yet *only* a little while *longer,* and he that shall come *to receive us unto himself* will come, and will not tarry.

39. "Now the just shall live by *his* faith, but if *any man* draw back, my soul shall have no pleasure in him," *saith the Lord.* (Habakkuk 2:4)

39. But we are not of them who draw back unto *condemnation and* perdition.But *rather we are* of them that believe *on the word of God* to the *very* saving of the soul.

CHAPTER 11

1. Now, *genuine* faith is the *very real* substance of things hoped for, *and* the *invisible* evidence of things not seen.

2.   For by it the elders *of old* obtained a good report *of others and of God*.

3.   Through faith we understand that the worlds *of this universe* were framed by the word of God, so that *the* things which are *currently* seen, were not made of *the* things which do appear.

4.   By faith Abel offered unto God *the blood of an innocent lamb.* A more excellent sacrifice than *the fruits that came from a cursed ground, presented by* Cain. By *the* which he obtained witness that he was right-eous *in his obedience.* God testifying of his *acceptable* gifts, and by it he *even* being dead yet speaketh.

5.   By faith Enoch was translated *from off of this planet earth,* that he should not see *physical* death. And was not found *by men,* because God had trans-lated him *to another location within this universe.* For be-fore his translation he had this testimony, that he pleased God *because of his faith.(And God will bring him back as one of the Two Witnesses, that shall be on this earth during the days of Antichrist.)*

6.   But without faith *it is* impossible to please *him.* For he that cometh to God must believe that he *really* is, and *that* he is a *great* rewarder of *all of* them that diligently seek him.

7.   By faith Noah, being warned of God of things not seen as *of* yet, *(i.e. massive flood waters to cover the earth,)* moved with *godly* fear, *and* prepared an ark

of wood, to the saving of his *own* house*hold.*By the which *actions* he condemned the *rest of the* world, *which would not listen to his warnings,* and *he* became *the* heir of the righteousness *that comes only from God,* which *righteousness* is by faith.

8.   By faith Abraham, when he was called *by God* to go out *of the city of Ur, of the Chaldees,* into a place which he should after*wards* receive for an inheritance, obeyed *God.*And he went out *into the wilderness,* not knowing whither he went.

9.   By faith he sojourned in *Canaan,* the land of promise, as *in* a strange country, dwelling in tabernacles with Isaac and Jacob, the *blood covenant* heirs with him of the same promise.

10.   For he looked *earnestly* for a city *spoken of* which hath *solid* foundations, whose builder and maker *is* God.

11.   Through *her* faith also Sarah herself received strength to conceive seed, and was delivered of a *man*-child when she was *long* past *childbearing* age, because she judged him *to be* faithful who had promised.

12.   Therefore sprang *from* there, even of one, and him as good as dead, *so many individuals* as the stars of the sky in multitude, and as the sand which is by the seashore innumerable.

13. *And* these *believing servants* all died in faith, not having *actually* received the promises, but having *only* seen them afar off.And *they* were persuaded of, and embraced, and confessed *the fact* that they were *only* strangers and pilgrims on the earth.

14. For they that say such things *as these* declare plainly that they seek a*nother* country, *other than this planet.*

15. And truly, if they had been mindful of that from whence they came out, they might have *been tempted, and have* had *an* opportunity to have returned.

16. But now they desire *in their heart* a better *country,* that is, an heavenly *home.* Wherefore God is not ashamed to be called their God, for he hath *specifically* prepared for them a city, *called the New Jerusalem.*

17. By faith Abraham, when he was tried *by God,* offered up *his promised son* Isaac.And he that had received the promises *from God, in a visionary manner,* offered up his only begotten.

18. Of whom it was *prophetically* said that, "In Isaac shall thy seed be called." *(Genesis 21:1)*

19. *Abraham* accounting that God *was* able to raise *him* up *again,* even from the dead. From whence also he *had* received him in a figure.

20.   By faith Isaac *prophetically* blessed Jacob and Esau concerning things *that were* to come.

21.   By faith Jacob, when he was a dying, blessed both *of* the sons of Joseph. And worshipped *God*, *while* **leaning** upon the top of his staff.

22.   By faith Joseph, when he *finally* died, made mention of the departing of the children of Israel *from the bondage of servitude.* And gave *a* commandment concerning his *own* bones,*that they should not be left in the land of Egypt.*

23.   By faith Moses, when he was born, was hid-*den* three *full* months of his parents,because they saw *that he was* a proper child. And they were not afraid of the king's commandment *to slay all of the male children that were born.*

24.   By faith Moses *himself*, when he was come to *his adult* years, refused to be called the son of Pharaoh's daughter *any longer.*

25.   Choosing rather to suffer *servitude*-affliction with the people of God, than to *continue to* enjoy the pleasures of sin for a season.

26.   Esteeming the reproach of Christ greater riches than the treasures *that arefound* in Egypt, for he had *a* respect unto the *genuine* recompense of the reward.

27.   By faith he *ultimately* forsook Egypt, not fearing the *stirred* wrath of the king. For he endured *and continued*, as seeing him who *at this time* is invisible.

28.   Through faith he kept the Passover *instructions*, and the sprinkling of *the lamb's* blood *as he was commanded*, lest he that destroyed the firstborn *of the land of Egypt*, should *be able to* touch them..

29.   By faith they passed *safely* through the Red Sea, *walking* as *if* by dry *land.* Which *when* the Egyptians *were* assaying to do *they* were *all* drowned.

30.   By faith the walls of *the city of* Jericho fell down *flat*, after they were *marched around, and* compassed about *by the men of Israel for* seven days.

31.   By faith the harlot Rahab, *who lived within the city walls*, perished not with *all of* them that believed not, when she had received the spies *of Israel* with peace.

32.   And what *else* shall I more say? For the time *and the space* would fail me to tell *you* of *the exploits of* Gideon, and *of* Barak, and *of* Samson, and *of* Jephthah. *Of the psalmest* David also, and *of* Samuel, and *of all of* the *other* prophets *of God.*

33.   Who through *their* faith subdued kingdoms, wrought righteousness, obtained promises, *and* stopped the mouths of lions.

34.   *They* quenched the violence of fire, escaped the edge of the sword, *and* out of weakness were

made strong. *They* waxed valiant in fight, *and* turned to flight the armies of the aliens.

35. *Some* women received their dead *children* raised *back* to life again. And others were tortured, not accepting deliverance, that they might obtain a better resurrection *when the time comes.*

36. And *still* others had trial*s* of *cruel* mocking*s* and scourging*s*, yea, moreover of *the torment of* bonds and imprisonment.

37. They were stoned *to death*, they were sawn asunder, *they* were tempted, *and* slain with the sword. They wandered about *clothed* in sheepskins and goatskins. Being destitute, *they were* afflicted, *and* tormented.

38. Of whom the world was not *really* worthy. They wandered in *the* deserts, and *in the* mountains, and *hid in the* dens and *the* caves of the earth.

39. And these all, having obtained a good report *from others,* through *their demonstrated* faith, received not the promise *of the Lord.*

40. God having provided, *within the whole of the process of time,* some better thing for us, *and* that they without us should not be made perfect.

CHAPTER 12

1.   Wherefore, *my beloved brethren,* **seeing** *that today* we also are compassed about with so great a cloud of witnesses, *of those who have followed Christ Jesus,* let us lay aside every weight, and the sin*s* which doth so easily beset *us,* and let us run with patience the race that is set before us.

2.   Looking unto Jesus *our Lord, who is* the author and *the* finisher of faith *itself.* **Who for the joy** that was set before him*, of redeeming Mankind unto God,* endured the cross *of Calvary,* despising the *imposed* shame, and is *now* set down at the right hand of the throne of God . . . *as a Man.*

3.   For consider him that endured such *a* contradiction of sinners against himself *while he was yet on this earth,* lest ye be*come* wearied and faint in your minds.

4.   Ye have not yet *personally* resisted *temptation* unto blood, striving against sin.

5.   And *it would seem that* ye have forgotten the exhortation which speaketh *expressly* unto you as unto children, "My son, despise not thou the chastening of the Lord, nor faint when thou art rebuked of him,

6.   For whom the Lord loveth, he chasteneth, and scourgeth every son whom he receiveth." *(Proverbs 3:11-12)*

7.   If ye *are then willing to* endure *such* chastening, God *will* dealeth with you as with sons, *and not simply as servants.* For what son is he, whom the father *of that son,* chasteneth not?

8.   But if ye be without chastisement, whereof all *legitimate children* are partakers, then are ye *in truth* bastards, and not *really* sons.

9.   Furthermore, we have had *our earthly* fathers of our flesh, which corrected *us when we needed it,* and we gave *unto* **them** *the* reverence *that they deserved.* Shall we not much rather be in subjection unto the Father of *our* spirits, and live?

10.   For they verily for *only* a few days chastened *us* after their own pleasure. But he *is chastening us* for **our own** profit, that **we** might be partakers of his holiness.

11.   Now, no chastening *or correction,* for the present *time* seemeth to be joyous, but *rather it seemeth* grevious. Nevertheless, afterward *if it is received,* it yieldeth the peaceable fruit of righteousness unto them which are exercised thereby.

12.   Wherefore lift up *to heaven* the hands which hang down, and *strengthen* the feeble knees,

13.   And make straight paths for your feet, lest that which is lame be *ultimately* turned out of the way. But let it rather be healed.

14. Follow peace with all *men,* and *purpose to perfect* holiness, without which *holiness,* no man shall see the Lord.

15. Looking *out* diligently *for one another,* lest any man *should* fail *in receiving and walking in the blessing* of the grace of God. Lest any root of bitterness springing up, *succeed in* troub*ling you,* and thereby many be*come* defiled.

16. *Or,* lest there *be* any fornicator, or profane person, as *Isaac's son* Esau *was,* who for one *carnal* morsel of meat, sold his birthright.

17. For ye know how that afterward, when he *thought that he* would have inherited the blessing, he was rejected *because that the blessing had already been given to Jacob his brother.* For he found no place of repentance *from his father Isaac,* though he sought it carefully with tears.

18. For ye are not come unto the Mount *Sinai* that might *not* be touched *because of a command from God,* and that burned with fire. Or unto *the* blackness, and *the* darkness, and *the* tempest.

19. And *to* the sound of a trumpet, and the voice of words *from heaven.* Which *voice even* they that heard *it* entreated that the word *of* God should not be spoken *un*to them anymore.

20. For they *who were gathered* could not endure that which was commanded, and if so much as a beast *shall even* touch the mountain, it shall be stoned *to death*, or thrust through with a dart.

21. And so terrible was the sight *of it*, *that even* Moses *himself* said, I exceedingly fear and quake.

22. But ye are come unto *the heavenly* Mount Zion, and unto the city of the living God, the heavenly *New* Jerusalem, and to an innumerable company of angels.

23. To the general assembly and *the* church of the firstborn, *the names of* which are written *down* in heaven. And to God, the Judge of all, and to the spirits of just*ified* men made perfect *through the finished work of the cross.*

24. And to Jesus, *who is* the mediator of the New *Christian Blood* Covenant. And to the *covenant* blood of sprinkling, that speaketh *much* better things than *that animal blood of* Abel.

25. See *to it* that ye refuse not him that speaketh *unto you.* For if they escaped not who refused him that spake on *the* earth, *namely Moses,* how much more **shall not we escape**, if we turn away from him that **speaketh** from heaven *namely Jesus our Lord.*

26. Whose voice then shook the earth *atop Mount Sinai,* but now he hath promised *through his prophets,* saying, "Yet once more I shake not the earth only, but also heaven." *(Haggai 2:6)*

27. And this *word,* "Yet once more," signifieth the removing of those things that are *able to be* shaken *at the renovation of the earth by fire*, as of things that are *temporal and* made, that those things which cannot be shaken *and are eternal* may remain, *such as the Kingdom of Heaven.*

28. Wherefore we receiving a kingdom which cannot be moved, let us have grace, whereby we may serve *our* God *faithfully and* acceptably, with reverence and godly fear.

29. For our God *is* a consuming fire, *that you do not want to fall into the hands of.*

CHAPTER 13

1. Let brotherly love continue *unabated.*

2. Be not forgetful to entertain strangers, for thereby some have entertained *holy ministering* angels, unawares *of who they are.*

3. Remember them that are *imprisoned and* in bonds, as *if you were* bound with them.*And* them which suffer adversity *and difficulties*, as being yourselves also in the *same, mystical* body *of Christ.*

4. Marriage *is* honourable in all *covenant giftings*, and the *marriage* bed *is* undefiled *from heaven's perspective.God* hath designed that within the covenant bond of marriage, *and only within the covenant bond, that sexual*

fulfillment between a man and a woman may be experienced and enjoyed.

5. **Let your** conversation *be* **without covetousness, and be** *ye* **content with such things as ye have. For he hath said, "I will never leave thee, nor forsake thee."** *(Joshua 1:5)(1 Chronicles 28:20)*

6. **So that we may boldly say, The Lord** *is* **my helper, and I will not fear what man shall do unto me.**

7. **Remember them which have the rule over you** *concerning spiritual things.* **Who have spoken** *and ministered* **unto you the word of God** *faithfully.* **Whose** *demonstrated* **faith follow, considering the end of** *their* **conversation;**

8. *The exaltation of the risen Lord of Glory,* **Jesus Christ,** *who is* **the same yesterday, and today, and for ever.**

9. **Be not carried about with divers and strange doctrines. For** *it is* **a good thing that the heart** *of a man* **be established with** *the* **grace** *that has been extended by a loving God.* **Not** *simply* **with** *various* **meats** *and drinks,* **which,** *in days gone by,* **have not profited** *any of* **them that have been** *so focused and* **occupied** *with the statute fulfillment* **therein.**

10. *Today,* **we have an** *heavenly* **altar, whereof they** *who continue to follow the Law of Moses* **have no right to**

eat *from;* which *continually* serve the tabernacle *that is still of this earth.*

11. For the bodies of those beasts *which are offered in sacrifice,* whose *shed* blood is brought into the *Holy of Holies* sanctuary by the High Priest *once a year* for *the atonement of* sin, are *ultimately* burned without the camp.

12. Wherefore, *in fulfilling the symbolism of that sacrifice, blessed* Jesus also, that he might sanctify the *whole of the Chosen* People *of God* with his own *shed* blood, suffered without the gate.

13. Let us *then leave our bondage to the Law of Moses, and the unprofitable animal sacrifices, and* go forth thereore unto him *who personally suffered for us* without the camp, *on the hill of Calvary,* bearing his reproach.

14. For here *on this earth* we have no continuing city *to look towards,* but we seek one to come *that is eternal, and has been promised.*

15. By him therefore, *that is, by Jesus Christ,* let us offer the *new* sacrifice of praise *un*to God continually;that is, the fruit of *our* lips giving thanks*giving* to his name.

16. But to *still continue to* do good, and to communicate *well,* forget not. For with such sacrifices *as these,* God is well pleased.

17. Obey them that have the rule over you *in any manner, whether spiritual or secular,* and submit

yourselves *willingly*. For they *are commissioned to* watch *out* for your souls, as they that must give *an* account*ing unto* God, that they may do it with joy *and delight*, and not with grief. For that *is going to be* unprofitable for you.

18.   Pray for us *please*. For we trust *that* we have a good *and sincere* conscience *before* God, in all things willing to live honestly.

19.   But I beseech *you* the rather to do this, that I may be restored *un*to you the sooner.

20.   Now the God of *all* peace, that brought *back* again from the *spiritually and physically* dead, our *precious* Lord Jesus; that great shepherd of *all of* the sheep *of his fold*; through the *priceless shed* blood of the everlasting *New Christian* Covenant;

21.   Make you perfect in every good work to *continue to* do his will *on this earth*. Working in you, *by the power of his Holy Spirit,* that which is wellpleasing *with*in his sight, through Jesus Christ, to whom *belongs the* glory for ever and ever.Amen.

22.   And I *humbly* beseech you, brethren, suffer the word of exhortation *that ye have received from me.* For I have written a letter unto you in *comparatively* few words.

23.   Know ye that *at this point in time,* **our** brother Timothy is *now* set at liberty. With whom, if he *shall* come shortly, I will see you.

24. Salute all *of* them that have the rule over you *spiritually*, and all *of* the *other* saints *as well.* They of *the believers here in* Italy salute you.

25. *The* grace *of our God be* with you all. Amen.

Epilogue

This is the third Biblical work with explosive enhancement. And once again, the enhancement is not inserted in order to change the text of the King James Translation of the Bible.

It is so important that the people of God have an understanding of the New Testament doctrines that have been established because of the finished work of Christ Jesus, upon the cross of Calvary.

Christianity must needs break away from centuries of tradition that is still occurring during these last days of the pre-Tribulation, falling away, travesty spoken of within II Thessalonians, chapter 2, verse 3—if we are really going to have any significant impact upon a lost and dying world.

We need to know who we are in Christ, and then purpose to rise to the occasion and engage in the spiritual warfare that is all around us.

The Book of Hebrews is also a major doctrinal work concerning post-resurrection realities. It does not present a Jesus, plus works, venue. Nor does it present a Jesus, plus Law of Moses, venue. It does not present a Jesus plus *anything* venue. It just presents a total faith in Jesus, and what he did, venue. And we cannot add to it, or take away from it. We can only accept and receive it, or reject it.

We really need to know what it says, and not just what we think it says, or what someone else says that it says. May the blessing of God be upon you, always.

Maranantha!

Meet the Author

By-The-Book Ministries, Inc. began in 2001 as a teaching outreach. Rob E. Daley has been gifted by God to be able to explain biblical truths in an easy to understand manner.

Many have been blessed by his teaching style.

Rob was saved and filled with the Holy Spirit in 1978 and has been instructed by the greatest teacher of all—the Spirit of Truth Himself. Rob is an ordained minister with the Assemblies of God International Fellowship and has pastored in various churches over the past 34 years.

It is the desire of this ministry to see the body of Christ solidly taught, and grow up into the things of the Lord. Rob is available for seminars, retreats, conventions, etc.

Rob can be reached at:

thedaleys@bythebookministries.org

http://robdaleyauthor.com

www.ingramcontent.com/pod-product-compliance
Lightning Source LLC
Chambersburg PA
CBHW020952030426
42339CB00004B/64